# Major Wolcott's
## *List*

# Major Wolcott's *List*

*Major Wolcott's List Firearms Used in the*

*Johnson County, Wyoming, Cattle War of 1892*

William N. Hockett

©2024

Cover photo courtesy of Elak Swindell. Used with permission.

# Contents

# Acknowledgments

I would like to thank the following people and organizations who helped me to complete this project:

Tom Lindmier and Steve Mount, whose book *I See by Your Outfit* encouraged me to do this work;

Merz Antique Guns for use of many photos (https://www.merzantiques.com/);

Lock, Stock & Barrel Auctions for use of photos of the J. D. Mynett Colt SAA (https://lsbauctions.com/);

Elak Swindell for use of his photo of the Nate Champion bronze;

James Kattner for use of his photos;

Cam Gogsill for use of his photos; and

David Carter and Ron Paxton for use of photos of the Elliot Sharps rifle.

# Preface

This book has taken a journey of many years. I read about the Johnson County War sometime in the 1970s, after my parents gave me *The Gunfighters* from the Time-Life Old West series. In 1990, while assigned to the US Air Force, I was stationed at Ellsworth Air Force Base, near Rapid City, South Dakota. Only about two hundred miles from Rapid City—relatively close in the Great Plains and Rocky Mountain West! I was interested in regional history. I read the excellent *The War on Powder River* by Helena Huntington Smith. It gave me much more background and context on the invasion.

Down the street from my house in Rapid City lived Keith Cochran, an author and expert of regional history and Colt Single Action Army firearms. In one of his books, Mr. Cochran mentioned the Johnson County War and listed some serial numbers of Colt revolvers taken from the invaders. There was no mention of where he gained this information. Unfortunately, Mr. Cochran died in March 1995, while I was stationed in Iceland, and I was not able to find out anything else.

Years later, I learned that author Robert A. Murray had been doing some research in the National Archives record group 98 on the frontier army in Wyoming, when he came across documents that included the Johnson County War. As soldiers from Fort McKinney near Buffalo, Wyoming, ended the siege, it makes sense there was information in the National Archives. The efficient recordkeeping of the US Army included a list of firearms surrendered by the invaders. Murray published the list in the May 1967 issue of *Shooting Times* magazine, in an article called "The Arms of Wyoming's Cattle War."

Murray listed the guns by the owners' names in no particular order. No analysis or context was given, and no attempt was made to identify the model or its features. To me, a collector of antique firearms, this seemed like a great research opportunity. My goal has been to get the list published in a manner that will allow collectors and historians to use the information to improve knowledge of the invasion and the weapons used by the invaders. In addition, having the information in the list able to be retrieved either by owner's name or by make, model, and serial number might allow a lucky collector to find an historical heirloom.

Where possible in my research for this book, I have consulted the Winchester records in the Cody Firearms Museum at the Buffalo Bill Historic Center.

I expect this will be an ongoing project. As more information is discovered, I may revise and expand the book.

# Abbreviations

CFM           Cody Firearms Museum

SAA           Single Action Army revolver

WCF           Winchester Central Fire or Winchester Center Fire (Winchester naming convention for proprietary cartridges)

WSGA        Wyoming Stock Growers Association

# Firearms Definitions

bullet          The projectile fired from a weapon. It was made of lead during the 1890s.

carbine        A rifle with a shorter barrel, typically designed to be carried on horseback.

cartridge      A complete round capable of being fired in a weapon. It contains a brass or copper case, gunpowder, a primer, and a bullet.

revolver      A handgun using a revolving chamber to hold multiple cartridges. During the 1890s, it might also have been called a pistol.

rifle           A long-barrel firearm designed for precise shooting over long distances.

set trigger    A hair-trigger mechanism that allows a rifle to be fired with a very light pull of the trigger. The Winchester November 1890 catalog listed this as an extra feature on Winchester rifles, available at additional cost.

# Cartridge Nomenclature

Reloadable brass cartridges became available in the last thirty years of the nineteenth century. They were loaded with black powder (referred to as gunpowder) at the time of the Johnson County War. Winchester had its own naming convention for its cartridges. Other firearms manufacturing companies also had naming conventions. I will provide listing and information on the cartridges used in the Johnson County War. The cartridges listed here can be identified as being used in guns surrendered at the end of the invasion. Some of the guns surrendered, such as the Sharps and Martini rifles, have unknown cartridges.

Pistol-caliber cartridges, such as .38 Long Colt, .38 WCF, .44 WCF, and .45 Colt, came in boxes containing fifty rounds. Rifle-caliber cartridges, such as .40-60, .45-70, .45-90, and .40-82, came in twenty-round boxes.

- .38 WCF: This Winchester cartridge (today known as .38-40) actually used a .401"-caliber inside lubed bullet. It was introduced in the Model 1873 rifle and carbine in 1879. It was loaded with 40 grains of black powder and a 180-grain lead bullet. This cartridge is still being loaded today but is not as popular as its .44 WCF cousin.

- .38 Long Colt: This Colt centerfire cartridge was introduced in the 1870s and replaced a rimfire version. The Model 1877 Lightning double-action revolver used a 148-grain bullet and 21 grains of black powder, according to the November 1890 Winchester catalog. It was not a very potent round.

- .38 Peabody-Martini: The exact cartridge used for C. A. Campbell's Peabody-Martini rifle is unknown. Most likely, it was the .38 Ballard Extra Long. This was a centerfire adaptation of the older .38 Extra Long rimfire. It used a 150-grain bullet and 31 grains of black powder. This was less than some of the pistol cartridges and much less potent than any of the other rifle cartridges used by the invaders.

- .38-56 WCF: This Winchester cartridge was introduced in 1887 for the Model 1886 rifle. It used a 255-grain bullet with 56 grains of black powder. It was not popular but was used in two of the 1886 carbines carried by the invaders.

- .40 Sharps: Sharps made several variations of its .40-caliber cartridges. The most popular variant in the Sharps rifles at the time of the Johnson County War was probably the .40-70 2½-inch straight. Bullet weights and powder charges could vary with these rounds. It was common for shooters to load their own ammunition and customize the bullet and powder charges. The .40 Sharps 2½-inch straight cartridge was introduced in 1879. It used 70 grains of black powder and a 330-grain bullet.

Joe Elliot's Model 1874 custom sporting rifle was in .40-70 Sharps 2½-inch straight. It is unknown the exact chambering of Elias Whitcomb's Sharps Model 1878 rifle.

- .40-60 WCF: This Winchester cartridge was introduced in 1884 for the Model 1876 rifle and carbine. It used a 210-grain bullet with 60 grains of black powder. It was more powerful than the .44 WCF cartridge used in the lighter 1873 model. It was available into the 1930s.

- .40-82 WCF: This Winchester cartridge was introduced in 1886 for the Model 1886 rifle. It used a 260-grain bullet with 82 grains of black powder. It was a relatively popular cartridge. It was loaded by Winchester into the 1930s.

- .41 Long Colt: This Colt centerfire cartridge was introduced in 1877. It was introduced for the Model 1877 Thunderer double-action revolver. It used a 200-grain bullet with 21 grains of black powder. It was also offered in the single-action revolver. It was not a very potent round. It was used in the double-action 1877 Thunderer and one SAA carried by the invaders.

- .442 Webley: This British cartridge was introduced in 1868 for the Webley Royal Irish Constabulary revolver. It was not very powerful, with 15 to 19 grains of black powder and a 200- or 220-grain bullet.

- .44 Smith & Wesson Russian: This S&W cartridge was introduced in 1871 for the Model 3 Russian revolver. It used a 246-grain bullet and 19 grains of black powder. This cartridge was popular for many years and was developed into the .44 Special.

- .44 WCF: This Winchester cartridge (today known as .44-40) actually used a .429"-caliber inside lubed bullet. It was introduced in the Model 1873 rifle and carbine in 1873. It was loaded with 40 grains of black powder and a 200-grain lead bullet. It proved to be a very popular cartridge and was also available in Colt revolvers. Four Colt single-action revolvers were in this caliber used by the invaders. This cartridge is still loaded today.

- .44-60 Peabody: This proprietary cartridge was used in the Peabody-Martini rifles. It used a 396-grain bullet with 60 grains of black powder.

- .45 Colt: This proprietary cartridge of the Colt Patent Firearms Company was used in two different revolver models during the Johnson County War. The most common and popular by far was the Single Action Army revolver. The 1878 double-action model also chambered it. It was normally loaded with a 250-grain bullet and 40 grains of black powder in the 1890s. This was a very powerful revolver cartridge. It was introduced in 1873. It is still loaded by several ammunition companies.

- .45-60 WCF: This Winchester cartridge was introduced in 1879 for the Model 1876 rifle and carbine. It used a 300-grain bullet with 60 grains of black powder. It was loaded into the 1930s.

- .45-70 Government: This cartridge was introduced in 1873 for US Springfield rifles and carbines. It was introduced by Winchester for its Model 1886 lever-action rifle and carbine in 1886. Four of the 1886 rifles used by the invaders were in this powerful cartridge. It was nominally loaded with a .405-grain bullet and 70 grains of black powder. Other bullet weight combinations were available. This cartridge proved so popular it is still loaded today.

- .45-90 WCF: This Winchester cartridge was introduced in 1886 for the Model 1886 rifle. It used a 300-grain bullet with 90 grains of black powder. It was a popular cartridge in early 1886 rifles. It was also loaded into the 1930s.

# Overview of the Invasion

The Johnson County War took place in Wyoming in April 1892. I will only provide a brief overview, as the cited publications take a much more in-depth look at the subject. In essence, a group of powerful Wyoming cattlemen created a "death list" of small ranchers, cowboys, and others they considered a hindrance to large-scale ranching interests. These cattlemen belonged to the Wyoming Stock Growers Association (WSGA) and included the political, social, and economic elite of Wyoming. They included the governor, United States senators, judges, powerful businessmen, newspaper owners, and more. This was not a group any small rancher or cowboy would have wanted to buck heads against. In early April 1892, these cattlemen planned an invasion of Johnson County and started to look for the seventy men on the death list they had created. Informal leaders of the invasion were Major Frank Wolcott and Frank Canton.

R. S. Van Tassel, a member of the WSGA, went to Colorado in January 1892 to purchase horses for the expedition. The purchase was made in Colorado so it would not set off alarms in Wyoming.[1] Local citizens of Cheyenne and other Wyoming towns would have been suspicious of so many horses being purchased. Fifty-two horses were purchased for the expedition. The men outfitted in Cheyenne. The WSGA made sure accounts were set up at local gun and saddle shops. A doctor, two reporters, and three teamsters also accompanied the expedition. Three brand-new Studebaker wagons were purchased for transport.

Tom Smith, a former stock detective, went to Paris, Lamar County, Texas, to recruit mercenaries. As a stock detective, it had been his duty to work for the stock growers' association and hunt down and eliminate horse and cattle rustlers. Smith found twenty-five Texans who hired on for the invasion. They were told they would serve warrants (there never were any warrants). Pay was to be five dollars a day with expenses, and there was also a bonus for each man killed from the death list.[2] These men waited in Denver for final authorization and then traveled by train to Cheyenne.

One hired gun, George Dunning, was recruited in Nampa, Idaho, by H. B. Ijams. Ijams was not able to find any other men in Idaho to join the invaders. Ijams sent money to Dunning so he could get his revolver out of hock before he left for Wyoming. He then traveled to Cheyenne, Wyoming, and visited saddle and gun

1    Helena Huntington Smith, *The War on Powder River: The History of an Insurrection* (McGraw-Hill Book Company, 1966), 191.

2    Ibid., 192.

stores where the cattlemen had set up accounts. On April 3, 1892, he got a new Winchester Model 1886 rifle, caliber .45-90.[3] The serial numbers of his arms are unknown.[4]

Other members of the invading army also picked up firearms and ammunition in Cheyenne. Many of the arms on the list were produced between 1890 and 1892. This implies they were very new and recently acquired. As you review each man's name, you will see what arms he had and when they were made. Some of the invaders undoubtedly carried weapons they already owned. It appears most of the Texans got new rifles, so they probably didn't bring their own to Wyoming. Typically, cowboys didn't own rifles, as they were too expensive and were not routinely carried on the range. The cattlemen and stock detectives would have had greater access to rifle ownership due to their wealth and position. Frank Canton later claimed each man was ordered to carry five hundred rounds of rifle and pistol ammunition on the saddle.[5] This seems doubtful, as that would have been a very heavy weight for rider and horse to carry. Also, it would have been difficult to pack that much ammunition in saddlebags and belts.

After getting their horses and arms, the invading army moved north. The WSGA had hired a special train to take them from Cheyenne to Casper. The train left Cheyenne late on April 5, 1892. It arrived in Casper during the early morning hours of April 6. Then the men unloaded their horses and set off north toward Johnson County. While the men were having breakfast on April 6, some of the loosely picketed horses broke loose and ran off. They were apparently only tied to sagebrush. They were not hobbled, which would have been a standard practice to keep them from running away. It took several hours to recover the horses, and some were not found. This event added delays and put the invaders behind schedule. It's possible that was when A. R. Powers had the stock broken on his Peabody-Martini rifle. A rifle in a scabbard on a horse often suffers a broken stock if the horse rolls on it. A broken stock makes the rifle unusable.

The invading army was packing heavy with their three Studebaker wagons. A Studebaker wagon was able to carry up to 2,500 pounds of cargo with a six-hitch horse team. However, 2,000 pounds was a more normal load. This would have allowed some bedrolls, food, water, cooking and medical equipment, and possibly other gear and extra ammunition to go in the wagons. It's possible some of the invaders' rifles were carried in the wagons as well. It can be cumbersome to carry a full-size rifle, such as a Winchester, on horseback.

---

[3]   A. S. Mercer, *The Banditti of the Plains, or the Cattlemen's Invasion of Wyoming in 1892* (University of Oklahoma Press, 1958), 174.

[4]   John W. Davis, *Wyoming Range War: The Infamous Invasion of Johnson County* (University of Oklahoma Press, 2010), 136.

[5]   Frank M. Canton, *Frontier Trails: The Autobiography of Frank M. Canton*, ed. Edward Everett Dale (University of Oklahoma Press, 1966), 88–89.

The heavy loads slowed the pace of the expedition, and the invaders camped on April 6, well behind schedule. By noon on April 7, it began to snow, and they stopped only thirty miles north of Casper. By the evening of April 7, the mounted men had made it to D. R. Tisdale's ranch about sixty-five miles north of Casper. The wagons were far behind and were not expected until the next day. It must have been a miserable ride in the wind, cold, and snow on muddy roads.

While at Tisdale's ranch, Mike Shonsey, a stock detective, arrived and said some of the men on the death list were camped at the nearby KC Ranch. Among them were Nate Champion and Nick Ray. A disagreement took place between Wolcott and Billy Irvine on one side and Frank Canton and Fred Hesse on the other. Wolcott and Irvine wanted to detour to the KC Ranch to kill the rustlers, while Canton and Hesse thought they should stick to the original plan of heading for Buffalo, where most of the men on the death list were expected to be. A vote was conducted, and the invaders moved out during the night of April 8 toward the KC Ranch. Two men stayed behind with the wagons. Dr. Penrose and reporter Ed Towse were supposed to ride in the wagons the next day. While at Tisdale's ranch, the first man abandoned the expedition. H. W. "Hard Winter" Davis stayed at the ranch with Ed Towse. He said his horse was unable to go on.[6] As he was not at the surrender, H. W. Davis's arms are unknown.

The invaders rode on through the night in a snowstorm. While it was still dark, they halted four miles from the ranch so they could build fires and warm up. Several scouts went forward to reconnoiter the house. Major Wolcott ordered the men to surround the cabin. He placed men in the stable and in the brush and covered every side. The invaders were surprised to find a buckboard on the property. (A buckboard is a small, four-wheeled horse-drawn wagon, something like a modern-day pickup truck. It could carry two people and some cargo in the back and was normally drawn by a horse or mule.) The invaders were not expecting any visitors; however, the buckboard's presence meant there were unknown visitors at the cabin. The extra men were out-of-work cowboys acting as trappers. It was a way to make a few dollars in the long winter months, when there was little work for cowboys.

After a while, one of these men left the cabin with a bucket to get water. He was captured when out of sight of the cabin. Later, his partner came out of the cabin and was also captured. After a while, Nick Ray showed himself outside the cabin. He was shot by C. D. Brooks, known as the Texas Kid, whom Wolcott had ordered to fire first. Ray fell but started to crawl back to the house. Nate Champion fired from the door and pulled Ray inside. He managed to graze the Texas Kid on the cheek. Ray died several hours later, but Nate Champion held out until afternoon. Later, the invaders attempted to set the cabin on fire and were able to force Champion out. He

---

6    Smith, *War on Powder River*, 202.

was shot down and killed as he attempted to flee the flaming cabin. It's possible Nate Champion wounded three men during the siege. The documentation is limited. There is no question he fought well and died a brave man.

While the invaders were besieging the KC Ranch, they were spotted by several locals, who raced north to Buffalo to raise the alarm. As the townspeople learned of the events at the KC Ranch, riders went to outlying small ranches. Men started to gather in Buffalo and organize into posses. Late in the afternoon on April 9, the invaders headed toward Buffalo, where many men on the death list were known to reside.

The people in Johnson County were alerted by that time. As the invaders moved north, they were tracked by some of the locals who had formed into posses. An errant gunshot alerted the invaders they had been spotted. They changed horses at a ranch six miles north of the KC Ranch. They stopped at Fred Hesse's ranch at two o'clock in the morning on April 10 to have a rest. Within two hours, they were on the march again, and they finally stopped at the TA Ranch, which was about fourteen miles south of Buffalo. The invading force started toward Buffalo, but they found out that the town had been alerted and that a posse was on the way to meet them. They decided to fall back on the TA Ranch and make a stand there.

About that time, reporter Sam Clover and invader Richard M. Allen left the TA Ranch compound. Allen told the others he had big cattle payments due. Once away from the ranch, he started abandoning his arms and ammunition.[7] Invader William Irvine wrote later that the group feared Allen would be hanged if captured by a posse.

Once news about the invasion reached Buffalo, the locals turned out in droves to defend their ranches and homes. Many men came in from nearby ranches. These men elected Arapaho Brown as their leader and established a camp at a nearby ranch. Supporters from Buffalo brought out food and other provisions. By Monday, April 11, there were several hundred men surrounding the TA Ranch. On that day, the three wagons showed up and were captured by the besieging locals. Inside were found extra ammunition, dynamite, fuses, and handcuffs. Also found in Frank Canton's valise was the death list with the names of all the men who were to be killed.[8]

In Buffalo, merchants opened their stores to supply arms, ammunition, clothing, and food to any men going to the siege at the TA Ranch. Merchant Robert Foote was one of them and provided many posse members with arms, ammunition, and equipment.[9] By the end of the siege on Wednesday, April 13, about four hundred men surrounded the TA Ranch.

---

[7]   Davis, *Wyoming Range War*, 163.

[8]   Smith, *War on Powder River*, 217.

[9]   Davis, *Wyoming Range War*, 166.

The invaders improved the defenses at the TA Ranch by digging rifle pits and building redoubts. Their position was a strong one, as the buildings, barn, and outbuildings were made of heavy hewn logs. Rifle fire alone could not drive them out. The leaders of the posse had the dynamite they had captured from the wagons. They developed a plan to use the wagons to create an "ark of safety" where they could get close enough to the fortifications to throw the dynamite in. In the interim, they established breastworks that surrounded the TA Ranch buildings from all sides. Men were placed at each breastwork to cover the buildings the invaders occupied.

The invaders were pinned down for two days and suffered some close calls. Billy Irvine was hit in the foot and walked with a limp for several days. J. A. Tisdale was hit in the back with a spent bullet that left a large bruise. Texan Alex Lowther was injured by his own gun. He later died in the Fort McKinney hospital. The posse soon got the range and shot out all the windows of the ranch. They also killed several horses in the corral so the invaders would not be able to use them. Horses always suffer when humans fight one another.

By Wednesday morning, April 13, the invaders' friends had been able to summon help. Governor Barber got President Benjamin Harrison to declare a state of insurrection in Johnson County and have the US Army put a stop to the fighting. Troops from nearby Fort McKinney came to the TA Ranch. Through negotiation, the invaders agreed to surrender to them.

As part of the surrender, the invaders turned in all their arms and equipment to the army. Major Wolcott, as unofficial leader of the group, made a list of these arms and provided it to the government. This list is now in the National Archives.

After the surrender, the invaders' lawyers and wealth helped them escape responsibility. No one was ever convicted for the murders of Nate Champion and Nick Ray. It appears the invaders were later able to reclaim their firearms that had been turned in to the army. Several have turned up in private collections over the years, as will be noted in the following sections.

# Firearms Used in the Invasion

Arms used by the rustlers (settlers, small ranchers, and townspeople of Buffalo) and the Johnson County sheriff's posse are a bit vague. It is known that at least one Sharps rifle, caliber .45 2 $4/_{10}$ inch (noted as an eighteen-pound Sharps), was used by Old Dan Boone (real name Harmon Fraker) to fire at the invaders besieged in the TA Ranch. This rifle, a Model 1874, serial number 157738, is in the collection of the Jim Gatchell Museum in Buffalo, Wyoming.[10]

Buffalo merchant Robert Foote joined the posse surrounding the invaders with his own rifle, a .45-90-caliber Winchester Model 1886, serial number 37423, also in the Jim Gatchell Museum collection. It was made in 1889.

Also, Sheriff Red Angus's Colt SAA is in the collection of the Wyoming State Museum. Few other guns with provenance to the rustlers are known. According to an oral history recorded years later, posse member John J. Baker said the posse had arms inferior to the invaders'. The posse only had "ordinary guns and six guns," while the invaders had high-powered rifles. Baker meant that the posse members would not have had guns with the range and firepower to reach the invaders in the TA Ranch buildings.

Nate Champion owned a Winchester Model 1886 carbine. Nick Ray owned a Remington-Keene rifle. Both these rifles are now in the Wyoming Pioneer Memorial Museum in Douglas. We can presume these rifles were not at the KC Ranch cabin when Champion and Ray were murdered, or they would likely have smoke and fire damage.

On the other hand, the arms used by the invaders are well documented for historians and collectors, thanks to Major Wolcott's list. Major Frank Wolcott was the self-appointed leader of the invaders. When the invaders surrendered to the US Army, Major Wolcott presented a list of all firearms belonging to each man. The list shows make, caliber, and serial number of each man's arms, as well as cartridges and cartridge belts. The serial number, caliber, or make is missing or incomplete for some entries. This is probably the most complete list of firearms that can be documented as used in western gunfights. I count forty-three men who surrendered arms. Originally, fifty-two men were on the train from Cheyenne to Casper. Some of the men were noncombatants (reporters and a doctor), some were injured before the surrender, and some left the group before or after they got to the TA Ranch. The list of firearms surrendered is almost unique in the history of Old West gunfights.

---

[10]    Margaret Brock Hanson, ed., *Powder River Country: The Papers of J. Elmer Brock* (1981), 316.

In the entire history of the American West, this list is the most comprehensive by far. It is rare for specific firearms information to be recorded about a gunfight.

All the men who surrendered had long arms (rifle or carbine). A couple of men turned in an additional rifle or a shotgun. Some of the men did not have a pistol (revolver). It's possible the cattlemen didn't consider a revolver necessary, as they anticipated all the fighting would be at longer range, more suitable for rifles. This proved to be the case. Among the Texas cowboys, it would have been more common to carry a revolver.

In some cases, there are questions as to which model of Colt revolver some of the men carried. The serial numbers could be for the Single Action Army (SAA), the Model 1877 Lightning (.38 Long Colt) or Thunderer (.41 Long Colt), or the Model 1878 Double Action Frontier. The models of 1877 and 1878 are both double-action revolvers. Some of the serial numbers for these revolvers duplicate those of the Single Action Army of the same period, as each type was numbered as a separate series. In other words, there may be an SAA, an 1877, and an 1878 with serial number 11697. If the actual revolver model is not listed (in Major Wolcott's list, this serial number is just shown as a Colt in .45 caliber), then it could be an SAA or a Model 1878. Further research by obtaining factory letters would benefit historians.

Major Wolcott's list was originally published in an article titled "The Arms of Wyoming's Cattle War" by Robert A. Murray in the July 1967 issue of *Shooting Times* magazine.[11] Murray discovered the list in the US Army record group 98 in the National Archives. The list had each man's name (though the names were not in alphabetical order), his arms, and extra equipment, such as cartridge belts. This makes it somewhat difficult for a collector only interested in Winchester Model 1873 rifles, for example. I have created a table that lists the guns with each man's name, by type, and also in serial number order. This is to assist collectors and historians to easily see all the Winchester Model 1873 rifles, Colt revolvers, and so on. I have also created separate biographies that identify the roles of the invaders and provide any other information I have found. As you will see from the list, the predominant handguns were Colts, and the predominant rifles were Winchesters. This should be no surprise to collectors and historians of the Old West period. Note that no Marlin, Whitney-Kennedy, Colt Lightning magazine rifles, or Bullard rifles are in evidence. With the exception of six single-shot rifles (four Peabody-Martini and two Sharps), all the rest of the rifles are lever-action repeating rifles. This is significant because it means lever-action rifles were dominant and largely replaced earlier single-shot rifles, such as the Sharps.

---

11    Robert A. Murray, "The Arms of Wyoming's Cattle War," *Shooting Times*, July 1967, 40–44.

For as many of the Winchester rifles as was practical, I received serial number lookup requests from the Cody Firearms Museum. I provided the model number (for example, 1886) and serial number. The CFM staff looked up information from the Winchester warehouse records. They then provided information about whether it was a rifle or carbine, the barrel type (octagon or round), the type of trigger (plain or set), and any other information. None of the Winchester rifles and carbines had any special order or extra features, except for two 1886s with set triggers. Any information I received from the serial number research is included for each man in the list.

Most of the rifles used by cattlemen and stock detectives were high-power big-bore types, such as the Winchester models 1876 and 1886. Conversely, most of the Texans, who were hired as professional gunfighters, favored the Winchester Model 1873 rifles and carbines, many of which were in caliber .38 WCF (today known as .38-40). Since many of these Texans were outfitted in Cheyenne, it's possible they were getting the arms that were left in stock after the cattlemen and detectives got first choice. There are sixteen Model 1873 rifles and carbines: eleven are carbines, three are rifles, and two cannot be determined because the last digit is missing in the serial number. Ten are in .44 WCF, and the other six are .38 WCF. Two of the rifles have octagon barrels, and one has a round barrel. All of them have standard wood-and-barrel configurations. No extra features are in evidence.

To put the costs of these guns into context, in the late nineteenth century, a typical cowboy or laborer made one dollar a day. To purchase a Winchester rifle and Colt revolver would have been more than a month's wages for a working man.

The Winchester Model 1873 was the firm's first centerfire production rifle. It was popular on the western frontier, as it was light, compact, and reliable, and ammunition was readily available. Using .44 or .38 WCF cartridges that could be reloaded was another convenience. Reloading tools, bullet molds, and powder were available for shooters to load their own ammunition. The standard barrel length for 1873 carbines was twenty inches, and they held twelve cartridges. Standard barrel length for 1873 sporting rifles was twenty-four inches, either round or octagon, and they held fifteen cartridges. The octagon barrel was listed at $19.50, while the round-barrel version was listed at $18.00 in Winchester's November 1890 catalog.[12] On sporting rifles, round barrels were cheaper, but octagon barrels were more traditional and popular with buyers. All carbines had round barrels.

A bonus for the Winchester Model 1873 was that it used ammunition that could also be used in Colt SAA revolvers. During the Johnson County War, only two of the invaders considered it a requirement to have the

---

[12] *Winchester's Repeating Fire Arms* (November 1890): 6.

six-shooter and rifle in the same caliber: Texans W. A. Wilson and K. Pickard. Each of these men had an 1873 carbine in .44 WCF as well as a Colt Frontier Six Shooter also in .44 WCF.

Young C. D. Brooks, known as the Texas Kid, was the invader reputed to have fired the first shot that hit Nick Ray as he emerged from the cabin. The Kid was using a Winchester Model 1873 carbine in .38 WCF.

Three Winchester Model 1876 rifles and carbines are on the list. One is a .40-60-caliber round-barrel rifle belonging to G. R. Tucker. Major Wolcott carried a .40-60 carbine. Fred Hesse carried a .45-60 carbine. Some .45-75 shell casings, as used in the Model 1876, were found on the TA Ranch during an archaeological excavation by Elmer Brock. It's possible they may have come from a rifle that belonged to one of the injured men or to Richard M. Allen, who left the TA Ranch before the surrender and abandoned his weapons along the way.

The Model 1876 was the firm's second production centerfire rifle and was introduced at the 1876 Centennial Exhibition in Philadelphia. It was Winchester's first production high-power big-bore rifle. It was meant to compete with the Sharps, the Remington, and other high-power single-shot rifles. The first production models reached the market in the summer of 1877. The earliest production rifles were made in caliber .45-75 Winchester, which used a 350-grain bullet backed by 75 grains of black powder in a short, tapered case. It was marketed as having as much power as the US government's .45-70 cartridge. The case was shorter than the government cartridge so it would feed correctly through the rifle's repeating action. Winchester followed with .45-60, .50-95 Express, and .40-60 cartridges in later years. The .45 cartridges were by far the most popular, with the .40-60 coming in third place. All were considered adequate for any North American big game.

The 1876 rifle and carbines used by the invaders have standard wood-and-barrel configurations. No extra features are in evidence. The standard barrel length for 1876 carbines was twenty-two inches, and they would carry nine cartridges. Standard barrel length for 1876 rifles was twenty-eight inches, either round or octagon. They would hold twelve cartridges. The round-barrel rifle was listed at $19.50 in Winchester's November 1890 catalog. The 1876 carbine listed for $19.00.

The 1873 and 1876 models were the last Winchester repeating rifles to use toggle-link technology first developed in the 1850s by Smith & Wesson. It was later used on the unsuccessful Volcanic rifle and pistol. It was again used in the successful Henry rifle and later Model 1866. By the time the 1873 and 1876 had been introduced, the toggle-link design was at the limits of its technology. John M. Browning's design that became the 1886 model was purchased by Winchester, who then manufactured the guns. The design of the Model 1886 was lighter, simpler, and stronger. It was made into the twentieth century.

Nineteen of the long guns used by the invaders were the venerable Winchester Model 1886 rifle and carbine, already popular just more than five years after its market debut. The most popular chambering among the invaders in the 1886 was the .45-90. There were two 1886 carbines, both in .38-56 caliber. There was one round-barrel rifle, and the remainder were octagon-barrel rifles. As with other Winchester rifles, round barrels were less expensive, but octagon barrels were more popular with buyers. Two of these rifles have a set trigger. This was a special-order item. There were nine rifles in .45-90, four in .45-70, four in .40-82, and the two carbines in .38-56. The 1886 rifle and carbines have standard wood-and-barrel configurations. No extra features are in evidence, except for two rifles with set triggers. The standard barrel length for 1886 carbines was twenty-two inches. Standard barrel length for 1886 rifles was twenty-six inches, either round or octagon. They would hold nine .45-70 cartridges or eight .40-82 or .45-90 cartridges. The octagon-barrel rifle listed for $21.00, and the round-barrel rifle was listed at $19.50 in Winchester's February 1890 catalog.[13] The 1886 carbine listed for $19.00. The set trigger was a $3.00 extra order feature.

Note also that four cattlemen used the Peabody-Martini single-shot rifle, in .38 or .44 caliber. This rifle, designed by an American, proved much more popular in the British empire. The exact model and configuration of these rifles are unknown. They were probably sporting rifles.

Two men used the Old Reliable Sharps single-shot rifle in .40 caliber. One of them is a Model 1874, and the other is a hammerless 1878 model. The Sharps had a time-tested and reliable action. The company went bankrupt in 1881, so these guns were purchased years earlier or on the secondary market. The Model 1874 was carried by detective Joe Elliot. The other Sharps was carried by Elias Whitcomb, who was the oldest member of the invaders. Sharps rifles had proven themselves on the frontier since the 1850s. They were somewhat obsolete by 1892.

The Colt Single Action Army revolvers (SAA or Peacemaker) on the list were all made prior to 1893. Collectors today refer to guns from that period as "black powder" frame models. It wasn't until the first decade of the twentieth century that Colt started approving these guns for the new smokeless powder.

Eventually, more than 300,000 Colt Single Action Army revolvers had been made by the time production ceased just prior to World War II. At the time of the Johnson County War, about 145,000 had been produced. In a single-action revolver, cocking the hammer back with the thumb moves a fresh chamber into line with the barrel. Pulling the trigger only releases the hammer. One must cock it manually for each shot by pulling back the hammer.

---

[13] *Winchester's Repeating Fire Arms* (November 1890): 30.

At the time of the Johnson County War, the cylinder base pin was secured with a screw that came up diagonally from the bottom of the frame. Three barrel lengths were considered standard for the SAA during that time period. The earliest and most traditional was 7½ inches. It allowed a longer sight radius and was the configuration of the SAAs bought by the US Army. It was popular with civilians as well. Colt subsequently released 5½-inch and 4¾-inch barrels. The 4¾-inch was especially prized for its balance and compact size. Of the Colt SAAs surrendered by the invaders, twenty-three were in .45 Colt, four were in .44 WCF, and one was in .41 Colt.

At least three of the Colt SAA revolvers used by the invaders are existent in private collections as of 2018. SAA serial number 118765 was carried by J. A. Garrett, a Texan, and now exists with a barrel cut to 4¾ inches and nickel finish. SAA serial number 135929 was carried by J. D. Mynett, a Texan, and is a 4¾-inch barrel with full factory engraving and blue finish. He must have been proud of such a fine revolver. The fact that these revolvers were eventually sold by the descendants of the original owners lends credence to their being returned by the army when the regulators were released.

Colt introduced double-action revolvers in 1877. A double-action revolver cocks the hammer and moves the cylinder to the next chamber by a pull of the trigger. The Model 1877 (Lightning in .38 Long Colt or Thunderer in .41 Long Colt) proved somewhat popular due to its small size. It could be carried in a coat pocket in the shorter-barrel variations. It appears that five men carried Model 1877 revolvers. Note that all the men who carried this model were cattlemen or detectives. None of the Texans carried it. The Model 1877 was considered a pocket model, and it was not available in the large .44 WCF or .45 Colt cartridge.

Colt followed with another double-action revolver in 1878 called the Omnipotent. This was a full-size gun of similar proportions to the SAA. It was available in the popular large-bore cartridges, such as .44 WCF and .45 Colt. During the invasion, three cattlemen and one Texan carried this revolver. All four were in .45 Colt. As you will see by looking at the list by type of firearm model, these double-action revolvers were not nearly as popular with the invaders as the older single-action model. Simplicity, reliability, and tradition made the single-action Colt popular well into the twentieth century.

The seven stock detectives in the expedition were all veterans of numerous skirmishes, both inside and outside the law. The Winchester Model 1886 was used by six of them, with Joe Elliot opting for the old standby Sharps single shot. Five of the detectives surrendered Colt SAA revolvers. Frank Canton surrendered an unknown revolver. Based on the serial number, it was probably an SAA in .45 Colt. Stock detective Ben Morrison turned in thirty-four revolver cartridges but no revolver. My guess is that he secretly kept it.

Each one of the invaders whose name ended up on the list had firearms that tell a story. Invaders who did surrender their arms are listed here.

While studying the list, I have made my best guess as to what the arms were, based on manufacture, serial number, and caliber. A Winchester .44-caliber rifle with serial number 197923 is a Model 1873. It cannot be an 1866 rifle, as the serial numbers didn't go that high. It can't be a Model 1876 or Model 1886, as they were not manufactured in this caliber. It can't be a Model 1892, as that model had not been commercially introduced at the time of the invasion.

Some of the firearms cannot be identified because not enough information is available. These include the Webley .44 revolver and the Smith & Wesson .44 revolver. I think it probable that the Webley was a Royal Irish Constabulary model or the British Bull Dog model.

The Smith & Wesson is equally hard to identify. It could be any of the .44 single actions, such as the .44 Model 3 American, .44 Model 3 Russian, or .44 New Model 3. It could also be a double-action .44.

# Arms Surrendered

The following cattlemen surrendered arms. I have included birth, death, and other dates if known. Few of these men have photos available.

**A. D. Adamson**: Adamson was from southern Wyoming and was a ranch manager of the Ferguson Land & Cattle Company. He turned in a Winchester .44-caliber Model 1873, SN 197923, with sixty cartridges and a .45-caliber Colt revolver, SN 11697, with a belt of cartridges. Based on the serial number, this revolver could be an 1878 double-action (probable) or a single-action army model (possible but unlikely). According to records in the CFM, this Winchester 1873 round-barrel rifle went to the warehouse on March 16, 1886, and was shipped out on April 24, 1886, to order number 6037. If the revolver is a Model 1878, it was made in 1883. If it is an SAA, it was made in 1874.

**G. A. Campbell**: Campbell owned a ranch in Converse County but lived in Cheyenne. He surrendered a .38-caliber Peabody-Martini rifle, SN 10805. He also turned in a .45-caliber Colt Model 1878 double-action revolver, SN 17632, made in 1886. A cartridge belt and holster were also surrendered.

**W. J. Clark**: Clark was water commissioner for Johnson County. It is unknown why he joined the vigilantes, since he was not a cattleman. He surrendered a .38-caliber Winchester Model 1873 rifle, SN 363142. According to records in the CFM, this Winchester 1873 octagon-barrel rifle went to the warehouse on December 18, 1890, and was shipped out on January 29, 1891, to order number 33. He also turned in a .38-caliber Colt Model 1877 Lightning double-action revolver, SN 11926, and a cartridge belt. Even though both these arms were caliber .38, they used different cartridges.

**Arthur B. Clarke**: Clarke was a rancher from Laramie County, Wyoming. He turned in a Winchester .44-caliber Model 1873, SN 26178?B, with 150 cartridges and a P. Webley & Sons .44-caliber revolver with fifty cartridges. The specific model of Webley is not known. It was probably a Royal Irish Constabulary model or possibly a British Bull Dog. According to records in the CFM, the Winchester 1873 rifle was made in 1888. The list shows an empty space after the 8 in the serial number, so I am unclear what that digit is supposed to be. It was common in the 200000s serial number ranges to have a letter *B* as a suffix. Its meaning is unclear, but it is not actually part of the serial number. The *B* suffix was not used in 20000s serial number ranges. No serial number is given for the Webley revolver.

**Frederic O. De Billier** (1857–1935): De Billier was a rancher from southeast Wyoming. He was educated at Harvard and resided in Cheyenne. He turned in a Martini .44-caliber rifle, SN 54763, and a .45-caliber Colt revolver, SN 103825. This SAA revolver was made in 1884. I don't know when the Martini rifle was made.

**Charles Ford**: Ford was foreman for the TA Ranch in Johnson County and a prominent rancher in Johnson County. He turned in a Winchester .45-70-caliber Model 1886 rifle, SN 47097, with sixty-two cartridges. According to records in the CFM, this Winchester 1886 octagon-barrel rifle went to the warehouse on July 24, 1890, and was shipped out on July 23, 1891, to order number 24769. It had a plain trigger and was in the same order as 47098 and 47100. The barreled action for this rifle was known to be in a private collection in 2022. The barrel has been cut to nineteen inches, and the stocks, magazine tube, and other parts are missing. Ford also turned in a Colt .45-caliber SAA revolver, SN 142387, with a cartridge belt (not full) and a shotgun. This SAA revolver was made in 1891.

**W. E. Guthrie**: Guthrie was a wealthy ranch owner, businessman, and politician. He surrendered a .45-70 Winchester Model 1886 rifle, SN 47100. According to records in the CFM, this Winchester 1886 octagon-barrel rifle went to the warehouse on July 24, 1890, and was shipped out on July 23, 1891, to order number 24769. He also turned in a .45-caliber Colt SAA revolver, SN 63501, made in 1881 and some cartridges.

**Fred G. S. Hesse** (1852–1929): Hesse was owner of the 28 Ranch and manager of the former 76 Ranch in Johnson County, near Buffalo. He turned in a Winchester Model 1876 carbine in .45-60, SN 46257, along with a cartridge belt and a Colt .45 Model 1878 revolver, SN 10163. According to records in the CFM, this Winchester 1876 carbine went to the warehouse on August 26, 1885, and was shipped out on August 29, 1885, to order number 112. The Model 1878 revolver was made in 1883.

**William C. "Billy" Irvine** (1852–1924): Irvine was a powerful and wealthy businessman and ranch owner. He was also a member of the livestock commission and one of the leaders of the invasion. He turned in a Winchester .45-70-caliber Model 1886, SN 47098. According to records in the CFM, this Winchester 1886 octagon-barrel rifle went to the warehouse on July 24, 1890, and was shipped out on July 23, 1891, to order number 24769. He also turned in cartridges but not a revolver. We can presume he didn't bother to carry one.

**F. H. Laberteaux**: Laberteaux managed the Hoe Ranch for wealthy owner Henry Blair, who lived in Chicago. He turned in a Winchester Model 1886 rifle in caliber .40-82, SN 50129. According to records in the CFM, this Winchester 1886 octagon-barrel rifle went to the warehouse on January 3, 1891, and was shipped out on March 13, 1891, to order number 1752. He also turned in a caliber .45 Colt SAA revolver, SN 102242. This revolver was made in 1884.

**Lafayette H. Parker**: Parker managed the Murphy Cattle Company. He surrendered a .38-56-caliber Winchester Model 1886 carbine, SN 62798, made in 1891. He also had two revolvers: a .45-caliber Colt SAA, SN 109305, made in 1884 and a .41-caliber Colt Model 1877 Thunderer double-action revolver, SN 17954, made in 1879. He also turned in three cartridge belts: one .41 Colt caliber, one .45 Colt caliber, and one .38-56 Winchester caliber. He was a well-armed cattleman.

**A. R. Powers**: Powers was a part owner of the Powers-Wilder Cattle Company in Johnson County. He turned in a Peabody-Martini .44-caliber rifle with a broken stock (no serial number listed). He also turned in a Colt .41-caliber revolver, SN 179?. Serial number information is incomplete. It must be an 1877 double-action model because the .41 Colt caliber was not offered in the SAA until the 114000 serial number range in 1885.

**Hubert E. Teschmacher** (1856–1907): Teschmacher was a wealthy part owner of a large ranching operation and member of the executive committee of the Wyoming Stock Growers Association. He turned in a .44-caliber Peabody-Martini rifle, SN 54745. He also turned in a Colt .45-caliber SAA revolver, SN 103825. This SAA revolver has the same serial number as the one turned in by F. De Billier, so there must be an error in the list.

**D. R. Tisdale**: D. R. Tisdale was a brother of John N. Tisdale and had a ranch on Willow Creek. He turned in a .45-90-caliber Winchester Model 1886 rifle, SN 58136. According to records in the CFM, this Winchester 1886 octagon-barrel rifle went to the warehouse on July 9, 1891, and was shipped out on January 4, 1892, to order number 17807. He also turned in a .41-caliber Colt Model 1877 double-action Thunderer revolver, SN 18766. This revolver was made in 1879.

**John N. Tisdale**: John N. Tisdale was a brother of D. R. Tisdale. He was living in Salt Lake City, Utah, but returned to Wyoming for the invasion. He turned in a .45-90-caliber Winchester Model 1886 rifle, SN 58153. According to records in the CFM, this Winchester 1886 octagon-barrel rifle went to the warehouse on July 8, 1891, and was shipped out on February 3, 1892, to order number 19373. He also turned in a bag of two hundred cartridges and a Smith & Wesson SA (single action?) .44-caliber revolver, SN 15897. This revolver was probably a New Model 3.

**W. B. Wallace**: Wallace was a British citizen visiting America, who apparently joined the invasion for unknown reasons. He met the man buying horses for the invasion in Longmont, Colorado. He turned in a

Winchester .44-caliber Model 1873 rifle, SN 54763. This rifle was made in 1880 and was one of the earliest Winchesters known in the invasion. He didn't turn in a revolver.

**Elias W. Whitcomb** (1831–1915): Whitcomb was the oldest member of the invaders and had come west in 1857. He lived in Cheyenne and had a ranch on Hat Creek. He surrendered a .40-caliber Sharps hammerless Model 1878 rifle, SN 15914. He also turned in a Colt .41-caliber SAA revolver, SN 140710. This revolver was made in 1891.

**Major Frank Wolcott** (1840–1910): Wolcott was another older member of the invasion force. He was a Civil War veteran and managed the VR Ranch. Wolcott had a reputation as a hothead and was one of the primary instigators of the invasion and the death list. He turned in a .40-60-caliber Winchester Model 1876 carbine, SN 52944. According to records in the CFM, this Winchester 1876 carbine went to the warehouse on April 8, 1886, and was shipped out the next day to order number 5337. He did not turn in a revolver.

The following stock detectives surrendered arms. These men were essentially professional killers, and they carried the best of the best when it came to firearms. Six of them carried Winchester Model 1886 rifles or carbines, the best available in April 1892.

**Frank M. Canton** (1849–1927): Canton's real name was Joe Horner, and he operated outside the law before coming to Wyoming. Never convicted, he was implicated in multiple killings in Wyoming. After the invasion, he turned in a .38-56-caliber Winchester 1886 carbine, SN 51980. This carbine was made in 1891. He also surrendered an unknown revolver, SN 55723, and two full cartridge belts. No caliber is listed for the revolver.

**W. S. "Quickshot" Davis**: Davis was a shotgun messenger for the stage line from Black Hills to Cheyenne in the 1870s and 1880s. During the invasion, he was W. C. Irvine's bodyguard. He surrendered a .40-82-caliber Winchester 1886 rifle, SN 8257. According to records in the CFM, this Winchester 1886 octagon-barrel rifle went to the warehouse on August 20, 1887, and was shipped out on September 2, 1887, to order number 22059. He also turned in a .45-caliber Colt SAA, SN 109511. This revolver was made in 1884. Davis also turned in a double-action Colt Model 1877 Lightning revolver in caliber .38, SN 14991. It was made in 1879 and was probably his backup gun.

**Phil DuFran**: DuFran was a stock detective and former ranch foreman. He surrendered a .45-90-caliber Winchester Model 1886 rifle, SN 49164. According to records in the CFM, this Winchester 1886 octagon-barrel rifle went to the warehouse on November 13, 1890, and was shipped out on January 19, 1891, to order number 24570. He also turned in a .45-caliber Colt SAA revolver, SN 144414. This revolver was made in 1891. It appears his weapons were almost new, probably obtained in Cheyenne before the invaders moved north. He had not actually accompanied the invaders but had been in Buffalo and joined them after they got to the TA Ranch. He was not held, as no charges were filed against him, and he was released.

**Joe Elliot**: Elliot was a detective and stock inspector. He was implicated in another killing and the attempted attack on Nate Champion before the invasion. He was out on bail for that assault at the time of the invasion. He surrendered a .40 2½-inch straight-cartridge Sharps Model 1874 sporting rifle, SN 162453. This rifle was modified by famed western gunsmith Frank Freund and has a pistol grip, checkering, and engraving. It is currently in a private collection. Elliot also turned in a .44-caliber Colt SAA (Frontier Six Shooter) revolver, SN 141080. This revolver was made in 1891.

**Ben Morrison**: Morrison turned in a .45-90-caliber Winchester Model 1886 rifle (no serial number listed). The list also says he surrendered 104 Winchester cartridges and thirty-four pistol cartridges. No pistol was listed as surrendered. Why would he have had pistol cartridges and no pistol? It makes me think that possibly the detectives were allowed to keep a sidearm. Or they kept one with a wink and nod.

**Mike Shonsey (possibly spelled Shaunsey)** (1864–1954): Shonsey was originally from Canada; he had worked as a ranch foreman previously. He surrendered a .45-90-caliber Winchester Model 1886 rifle, SN 58018. According to records in the CFM, this Winchester 1886 octagon-barrel rifle went to the warehouse on July 9, 1891, and shipped from the warehouse on August 13, 1891, to order number 9196. He also surrendered a .45-caliber Colt SAA revolver, SN 94587. This revolver was made in 1883.

**W. H. Tabor**: Tabor, a detective, turned in a .45-90-caliber Winchester Model 1886 rifle, SN 48917. According to records in the CFM, this Winchester 1886 octagon-barrel rifle went to the warehouse on November 11, 1890, and was shipped out on December 15, 1890, to order number 23020. He also turned in a .45-caliber Colt SAA revolver, SN 29768. This revolver was made in 1877, making it one of the earlier SAAs available for civilian sale.

# Hired Gunmen

These men came from the Paris, Lamar County, Texas, area. One man, George Dunning, was recruited in Idaho. It is highly likely some of them didn't have firearms of their own. Note that most of their arms have late serial numbers that were made in 1890–92. This most likely means they received them in Cheyenne before the invasion force headed north. A gun store owned by Peter Bergersen is listed in the Cheyenne business directory for 1889. It is likely the guns were purchased at this store.

**William Armstrong**: Armstrong surrendered a .38-caliber Winchester Model 1873 carbine, SN 345928. According to records in the CFM, this Winchester 1873 carbine went to the warehouse on July 10, 1890, and was shipped out on July 14, 1890, to order number 14549. He also surrendered a Colt .45-caliber SAA revolver, SN 144682. This revolver was made in 1892. It is almost sure that Armstrong got these weapons in Cheyenne as the invaders fitted out before heading north.

**Bob Barling**: Bob Barling was a brother to J. Barling. He turned in a .40-82-caliber Winchester Model 1886 rifle, SN 30284, along with sixty rifle cartridges. According to records in the CFM, this Winchester 1886 octagon-barrel rifle with set trigger went to the warehouse on June 12, 1889, and was shipped out on June 14, 1889, to order number 21772. A set trigger was a special-order option on Winchester rifles and uncommon in the Model 1886. It was a three-dollar option over the twenty-one-dollar list price. He also surrendered a .45-caliber Colt SAA revolver, SN 142792, and thirty cartridges. This revolver was made in 1891.

**J. Barling**: J. Barling was a brother to Bob Barling. He turned in a .45-90-caliber Winchester Model 1886 rifle, SN 60504. According to records in the CFM, this Winchester 1886 octagon-barrel rifle went to the warehouse on September 7, 1891, and was shipped out on October 5, 1891, to order number 12485. He also turned in a .45-caliber Colt SAA revolver, SN 139904. This revolver was made in 1891. J. Barling also turned in a cartridge belt and holster.

**F. M. Benford**: Benford surrendered a .38-caliber Winchester Model 1873 carbine, SN 362444. This carbine was made in 1890. Benford also turned in a .45-caliber Colt SAA revolver, SN 142781. This revolver was made in 1891. He also had twenty-seven .38 Winchester cartridges and twenty revolver cartridges.

**C. D. Brooks:** Brooks was reputed to have fired the first shot that hit Nick Ray at the KC Ranch. He turned in a .38-caliber Winchester Model 1873 carbine, SN 386977. According to records in the CFM, this Winchester 1873 carbine went to the warehouse on June 11, 1891. There is no shipping information. He also had a .45-caliber Colt SAA revolver, SN 120241. This revolver was made in 1887. Some sources list his name as D. E. Booke, but I have listed it as it is shown in the primary references.

**Buck Garrett:** Garrett surrendered a .44-caliber Winchester Model 1873 carbine, SN 66960, made in 1881. He also turned in a .45-caliber Colt SAA, SN 145105, made in 1892. This SAA must have been hot off the Colt factory floor and rushed out west. He also turned in a belt and scabbard.

**J. A. Garrett:** Garrett turned in a .44-caliber Winchester Model 1873 rifle, SN 327276. According to records in the CFM, this Winchester 1873 octagon-barrel rifle went to the warehouse on January 11, 1890, and was shipped out on February 7, 1890, to order number 10208. Garrett also had a .45-caliber Colt SAA, SN 118765, made in 1886 and also surrendered a cartridge belt and scabbard. This revolver survives today in a private collection.

**Alex Hamilton:** Hamilton surrendered a .44-caliber Winchester Model 1873 carbine, SN 179707. This carbine was made in 1885. He also turned in a .45-caliber Colt SAA revolver, SN 112378, made in 1884, along with a belt and cartridges.

**J. C. Johnson:** Johnson turned in a .45-90 Winchester Model 1886 rifle, SN 60038. According to records in the CFM, this Winchester 1886 octagon-barrel rifle went to the warehouse on August 29, 1891, and was shipped out on October 29, 1891, to order number 13836. He also turned in a rifle belt with cartridges. He also turned in a .45-caliber Colt SAA revolver, SN 117844, along with a belt and scabbard. This revolver was made in 1886. It survives today in a private collection.

**William Little:** Little surrendered a .38-caliber Winchester Model 1873 rifle, SN 345860. According to records in the CFM, this Winchester 1873 carbine went to the warehouse on July 10, 1890, and was shipped out on August 5, 1890, to order number 15572. He also turned in a .45-caliber Colt SAA revolver, SN 143567, made in 1891 and one cartridge belt.

**M. A. McNally:** McNally surrendered a .44-caliber Winchester Model 1873, SN 32733?. Even with the last digit missing, it's known this Model 1873 was made in 1890. We don't know the exact configuration without the missing digit. He also turned in a .45-caliber Colt SAA, SN 143609, made in 1891.

**J. D. Mynett**: Mynett surrendered a .45-90-caliber Winchester Model 1886 rifle, SN 42164, shipped on April 29, 1890. He also turned in a beautiful, factory-engraved pearl-gripped .45-caliber Colt SAA, SN 135929, made in 1890. This one-of-a-kind Colt survives today in a private collection, although the grips have been changed to stag. Mynett also turned in a cartridge belt.

**K. Pickard**: Pickard surrendered a .44-caliber Winchester Model 1873 carbine, SN 251649. According to records in the CFM, this Winchester 1873 carbine went to the warehouse on October 28, 1887, and was shipped out on November 1, 1887, to order number 1121. He also turned in a .44-caliber Colt Frontier Six Shooter, SN 116184, made in 1885 and 120 cartridges. Pickard was one of only two members of the vigilantes to have a rifle or carbine and a revolver in the same caliber. Based on the manufacture dates of his arms, it appears he brought them from Texas.

**B. C. Schultz**: Schultz surrendered a .44-caliber Winchester Model 1873 carbine, SN 335042. According to records in the CFM, this Winchester 1873 carbine went to the warehouse on March 20, 1890, and was shipped out on March 20, 1890, to order number 10395. He also turned in a .45-caliber Colt SAA revolver, SN 143314, made in 1891, along with twenty-seven Winchester cartridges and sixty-nine revolver cartridges.

**G. R. Tucker**: Tucker was well equipped with weapons. He surrendered a .40-60-caliber Winchester Model 1876 rifle. According to records in the CFM, this Winchester 1876 round-barrel rifle went to the warehouse on September 10, 1886, and was shipped out on September 14, 1886, to order number 10261. Tucker also had a .40-82-caliber Winchester Model 1886 rifle, SN 59760. According to records in the CFM, this Winchester 1886 round-barrel rifle went to the warehouse on August 19, 1891, and was shipped out on August 26, 1891, to order number 9838. Tucker also turned in a .45-caliber Colt Model 1878 double-action revolver, SN 293, made in 1878. Tucker surrendered 107 Winchester cartridges. It is possible Tucker was carrying a rifle that belonged to one of the wounded men.

**S. S. Tucker**: S. S. Tucker's name is sometimes shown as D. S. Tucker. I have listed his name the way it is shown on the list. He surrendered a .45-70 Winchester Model 1886 rifle, SN 48143. According to records in the CFM, this Winchester 1886 octagon-barrel, set-trigger rifle went to the warehouse on December 24, 1890, and was shipped out on September 4, 1891, to order number 10307. A set trigger was a special-order option on Winchester rifles and uncommon in the Model 1886. It was a three-dollar option over the twenty-one-dollar list price. He also turned in a .44-caliber Colt Frontier Six Shooter, SN 97623, made in 1883, along with a full cartridge belt.

**B. Wiley**: Wiley surrendered a .38-caliber Winchester Model 1873 carbine, SN 362439, made in 1890. He also turned in a .45-caliber Colt SAA revolver, SN 135184, made in 1890 and a cartridge belt.

**W. A. Wilson**: Wilson surrendered a .44-caliber Winchester Model 1873 carbine, SN 324793. According to records in the CFM, this Winchester 1873 carbine went to the warehouse on December 24, 1889, and was shipped out on December 24, 1889, to order number 7437. He also turned in a .44-caliber Colt Frontier Six Shooter, SN 141475, made in 1891. He was one of two men to have a longarm and a revolver in the same cartridge, in this case .44 WCF.

Two other Texans were wounded during the invasion, and their names are not on the list. Jim Dudley died at Fort McKinney after being shot in the knee by his own rifle after getting bucked off a horse at the TA Ranch. I don't know what happened to his weapons.

Alex Lowther was the other wounded Texan. He was crawling on the ground to maintain cover, when a cocked revolver in his waistband discharged, hitting him in the groin. He also later died at Fort McKinney. I don't know what happened to his weapons, and his name is not on the list.

Richard M. Allen was assistant manager of the Standard Cattle Company from Cheyenne and joined the invasion out of loyalty to the Wyoming Stock Growers Association. Allen and reporter Sam Clover, who also supported the invasion, left the vigilantes after arriving at the TA Ranch. Clover said Allen threw away his guns and ammunition so he would not be tied to the vigilantes.[14]

---

[14]   *Winchester's Repeating Fire Arms* (November 1890): 163.

# Bibliography

Brock Hanson, Margaret. *Powder River Country: The Papers of J. Elmer Brock*. Cheyenne: Frontier Printing, 1981.

Canton, Frank M. *Frontier Trails: The Autobiography of Frank M. Canton*. Norman: University of Oklahoma Press, 1966.

Davis, John W. *Wyoming Range War: The Infamous Invasion of Johnson County*. Norman: University of Oklahoma Press, 2010.

Flayderman, Norm. *Flayderman's Guide to Antique American Firearms and Their Values*. 8th ed. Iola: Krause Publications, 2001.

Madis, George. *The Winchester Book*. Brownsboro: Art and Reference House, 1985.

Mercer, A. S. *The Banditti of the Plains, or the Cattlemen's Invasion of Wyoming in 1892*. Norman: University of Oklahoma Press, 1958.

Murray, Robert A. "The Arms of Wyoming's Cattle War." *Shooting Times*, July 1967.

Smith, Helena Huntington. *The War on Powder River*. New York City: McGraw-Hill Book Company, 1966.

*Winchester's Repeating Fire Arms* catalog (November 1890).

**Table 1**

# Firearms by Make, Model, and Serial Number

| Name | Manufacturer | Model | Serial Number | Caliber | Made/ Date to Warehouse | Other Info | Extra Information | Role |
|---|---|---|---|---|---|---|---|---|
| **Revolvers** | | | | | | | | |
| J. N. Tisdale | Smith & Wesson | SA | 15897 | .44 S & W | - | - | | Cattleman |
| A. B. Clarke | Webley | ? | ? | .44 Cal. | - | - | | Cattleman |
| | | | | | | | | |
| A. R. Powers | Colt | M1877 | 179? | .41 Colt | - | Probably M1877 | | Cattleman |
| W. J. Clark | Colt | M1877 | 11926 | .38 Cal. | 1878 | Probably M1877 | | Cattleman |
| W. S. Davis | Colt | M1877 | 14991 | .38 Cal. | 1879 | Probably M1877 | | Detective |
| L. H. Parker | Colt | M1877 | 17954 | .41 Colt | 1879 | Probably M1877 | | Cattleman |
| D. R. Tisdale | Colt | M1877 | 18766 | .41 Colt | 1879 | Probably M1877 | | Cattleman |
| | | | | | | | | |
| G. R. Tucker | Colt | M1878 | 293 | .45 Colt | 1878 | Possibly SAA | | Texan |
| F. Hesse | Colt | M1878 | 10163 | .45 Colt | 1883 | Possibly SAA | | Cattleman |
| A. D. Adamson | Colt | M1878 | 11697 | .45 Colt | 1883 | Possibly SAA | | Cattleman |
| G. A. Campbell | Colt | M1878 | 17632 | .45 Colt | 1886 | Possibly SAA | | Cattleman |
| | | | | | | | | |
| W. H. Tabor | Colt | SAA | 29768 | .45 Colt | 1877 | - | | Detective |
| Ben Morrison | Colt | SAA | 50240 | .45 Colt | 1879 | - | | Detective |
| Frank Canton | ? | ? | 55728 | ? | - | Probably SAA | | Detective |
| W. E. Guthrie | Colt | SAA | 63501 | .45 Colt | 1881 | - | | Cattleman |
| Mike Shonsey | Colt | SAA | 94587 | .45 Colt | 1883 | - | | Detective |
| S. S. Tucker | Colt | SAA | 97623 | .44 WCF | 1883 | - | | Texan |
| F. H. Laberteaux | Colt | SAA | 102242 | .45 Colt | 1884 | - | | Cattleman |
| F. De Billier | Colt | SAA | 103825 | .45 Colt | 1884 | - | | Cattleman |
| L. H. Parker | Colt | SAA | 109305 | .45 Colt | 1884 | - | | Cattleman |
| W. S. Davis | Colt | SAA | 109511 | .45 Colt | 1884 | - | | Detective |
| Alex Hamilton | Colt | SAA | 112878 | .45 Colt | 1884 | - | | Texan |
| K. Pickard | Colt | SAA | 116184 | .44 WCF | 1885 | .44 WCF carbine | | Texan |
| J. C. Johnson | Colt | SAA | 117844 | .45 Colt | 1886 | - | Private collection | Texan |

| | | | | | | | | |
|---|---|---|---|---|---|---|---|---|
| J. A. Garrett | Colt | SAA | 118765 | .45 Colt | 1886 | - | Private collection | Texan |
| C. D. Brooks | Colt | SAA | 120241 | .45 Colt | 1887 | The Texas Kid | | Texan |
| B. Wiley | Colt | SAA | 135184 | .45 Colt | 1890 | - | | Texan |
| J. D. Mynett | Colt | SAA | 135929 | .45 Colt | 1890 | - | Private collection | Texan |
| J. Barling | Colt | SAA | 139904 | .45 Colt | 1891 | Brother to Bob | | Texan |
| E. Whitcomb | Colt | SAA | 140710 | .41 Colt | 1891 | - | | Cattleman |
| Joe Elliot | Colt | SAA | 141080 | .44 WCF | 1891 | - | | Detective |
| W. A. Wilson | Colt | SAA | 141475 | .44 WCF | 1891 | .44 WCF rifle | | Texan |
| Charles Ford | Colt | SAA | 142387 | .45 Colt | 1891 | - | | Cattleman |
| F. M. Benford | Colt | SAA | 142781 | .45 Colt | 1891 | - | | Texan |
| Bob Barling | Colt | SAA | 142792 | .45 Colt | 1891 | Brother to J. | | Texan |
| B. C. Schultz | Colt | SAA | 143314 | .45 Colt | 1891 | - | | Texan |
| William Little | Colt | SAA | 143567 | .45 Colt | 1891 | - | | Texan |
| M. A. McNally | Colt | SAA | 143609 | .45 Colt | 1891 | - | | Texan |
| Phil DuFran | Colt | SAA | 144414 | .45 Colt | 1892 | - | | Detective |
| Will Armstrong | Colt | SAA | 144682 | .45 Colt | 1892 | - | | Texan |
| Buck Garrett | Colt | SAA | 145105 | .45 Colt | 1892 | - | | Texan |

**Rifles**

| | | | | | | | | |
|---|---|---|---|---|---|---|---|---|
| W. B. Wallace | Winchester | 1873 | 54763 | .44 WCF | 1880 | Englishman | Carbine, 1 belt | Cattleman |
| Buck Garrett | Winchester | 1873 | 66960 | .44 WCF | 1881 | - | Carbine, 1 belt, holster | Texan |
| Alex Hamilton | Winchester | 1873 | 179707B | .44 WCF | 1885 | - | Carbine, 1 belt, ctgs. | Texan |
| A. D. Adamson | Winchester | 1873 | 197923 | .44 WCF | 3-16-1886 | 60 .44 WCF ctgs. | Rnd rifle,1 belt, ctgs. | Cattleman |
| K. Pickard | Winchester | 1873 | 251649 | .44 WCF | 10-28-1887 | .44 WCF revolver | Carbine, 120 ctgs. | Texan |
| A. B. Clarke | Winchester | 1873 | 26178?B | .44 WCF | 1888 | 150 .44 WCF ctgs. | 50 Webley ctgs. | Cattleman |
| W. A. Wilson | Winchester | 1873 | 324793B | .44 WCF | 12-24-1890 | .44 WCF revolver | Carbine, belt, scab. | Texan |
| J. A. Garrett | Winchester | 1873 | 327276B | .44 WCF | 3-17-1890 | - | Oct rifle, 1 belt, ctgs., scab. | Texan |
| M. A. McNally | Winchester | 1873 | 32733?B | .44 WCF | 1890 | - | - | Texan |
| B. C. Schultz | Winchester | 1873 | 335042 | .44 WCF | 3-20-1890 | 27 .44 WCF ctgs. | Carbine, 60 .45 Colt ctgs. | Texan |
| William Little | Winchester | 1873 | 345860 | .38 WCF | 7-10-1890 | - | Carbine, 1 belt | Texan |
| Will Armstrong | Winchester | 1873 | 345928B | .38 WCF | 7-10-1890 | - | Carbine, 1 belt, holster | Texan |

| | | | | | | | | | |
|---|---|---|---|---|---|---|---|---|---|
| B. Wiley | Winchester | 1873 | 362439 | .38 WCF | 1890 | - | | Carbine, 1 belt | Texan |
| F. M. Benford | Winchester | 1873 | 362444B | .38 WCF | 1890 | 27 .38 WCF ctgs. | | Carbine, 20 .45 Colt ctgs. | Texan |
| W. J. Clark | Winchester | 1873 | 363142 | .38 WCF | 12-18-1890 | - | | Oct rifle,1 belt | Cattleman |
| C. D. Brooks | Winchester | 1873 | 386977B | .38 WCF | 6-11-1891 | The Texas Kid | | Carbine | Texan |
| F. Hesse | Winchester | 1876 | 46257 | .45-60 | 8-26-1885 | - | | Carbine, 1 belt | Cattleman |
| Frank Wolcott | Winchester | 1876 | 52944 | .40-60 | 4-9-1886 | - | | Carbine | Cattleman |
| G. R. Tucker | Winchester | 1876 | 55201 | .40-60 | 9-14-1886 | Also had 1886 | | Rnd rifle | Texan |
| | | | | | | | | | |
| Ben Morrison | Winchester | 1886 | ? | .45-90 | ? | 104 .45-90 ctgs. | | 34 revolver ctgs. | Detective |
| W. S. Davis | Winchester | 1886 | 8257 | .40-82 | 9-2-1887 | - | | Oct rifle | Detective |
| Bob Barling | Winchester | 1886 | 30284 | .40-82 | 6-12-1889 | Brother to J. | | Oct rifle, set, 30 ctgs. | Texan |
| J. D. Mynett | Winchester | 1886 | 42164 | .45-90 | 4-29-1890 | - | | Oct rifle,1 belt | Texan |
| Charles Ford | Winchester | 1886 | 47097 | .45-70 | 7-24-1890 | Shotgun also | | Oct rifle, 1 belt (not full) | Cattleman |
| W. C. Irvine | Winchester | 1886 | 47098 | .45-70 | 7-24-1890 | | | Oct rifle, ctgs. | Cattleman |
| W. E. Guthrie | Winchester | 1886 | 47100 | .45-70 | 7-24-1890 | - | | Oct rifle, ctgs. | Cattleman |
| S.S. Tucker | Winchester | 1886 | 48143 | .45-70 | 12-24-1890 | - | | Oct rifle, set, 1 full belt | Texan |
| W. H. Tabor | Winchester | 1886 | 48917 | .45-90 | 11-11-1890 | | | Oct rifle, 3 belts, 142 ctgs. | Detective |
| Phil DuFran | Winchester | 1886 | 49164 | .45-90 | 11-13-1890 | - | | Oct rifle, 1 belt | Detective |
| F. H. Laberteaux | Winchester | 1886 | 50129 | .40-82 | 1-3-1891 | - | | Oct rifle, 1 belt, scab. | Cattleman |
| Frank Canton | Winchester | 1886 | 51980 | .38-56 | 1891 | - | | Carbine, 2 belts | Detective |
| Mike Shonsey | Winchester | 1886 | 58018 | .45-90 | 7-9-1891 | - | | 1 belt, holster, ctgs. | Detective |
| D. R. Tisdale | Winchester | 1886 | 58136 | .45-90 | 7-9-1891 | - | | Oct rifle, 1 belt, 60 ctgs. | Cattleman |
| J. N. Tisdale | Winchester | 1886 | 58153 | .45-90 | 7-8-1891 | - | | Oct rifle, 200 ctgs. | Cattleman |
| G. R. Tucker | Winchester | 1886 | 59760 | .40-82 | 8-19-1891 | Also had 1876 | | Rnd rifle, 107 ctgs. | Texan |

| | | | | | | | | |
|---|---|---|---|---|---|---|---|---|
| J. C. Johnson | Winchester | 1886 | 60038 | .45-90 | 8-29-1891 | - | Oct rifle, 1 belt, scab. | Texan |
| J. Barling | Winchester | 1886 | 60504 | .45-90 | 9-7-1891 | - | Oct rifle, 1 belt, holster | Texan |
| L. H. Parker | Winchester | 1886 | 62798 | .38-56 | 1891 | - | Carbine, 3 belts, holster | Cattleman |
| A. R. Powers | Martini | ? | ? | .44 cal. | ? | Broken stock | 1 full belt | Cattleman |
| C. A. Campbell | Martini | ? | 10805 | .38 cal. | ? | - | 1 belt, holster | Cattleman |
| H. Teschmacher | Martini | ? | 54745 | .44 cal. | ? | - | | Cattleman |
| F. De Billier | Martini | ? | 54763 | .44 cal. | ? | - | | Cattleman |
| E. Whitcomb | Sharps | 1878 | 15914 | .40 cal. | ? | 50 Sharps ctgs. | 50 .41 Colt ctgs. | Cattleman |
| Joe Elliot | Sharps | 1874 | 162453 | .40 cal. | Freund Sharps | - | 1 belt, holster, ctgs. | Detective |

# Illustrations

Figure 1: The Johnson County invaders, 1892. Photo public domain.

Figure 2: Colt Single Action Army revolver, .44 WCF caliber with 7½-inch barrel. Case-hardened frame and hammer with other parts blued. Standard finish for Colt revolvers. *Colt Frontier Six Shooter* roll-engraved on left side of barrel. Author's collection.

Figure 3: Colt Single Action Army revolver, .45 Colt caliber with 4¾-inch barrel. Author's collection.

Figure 4: J. D. Mynett's Colt Single Action Army revolver, .45 Colt caliber with 4¾-inch barrel. Photo courtesy of Lock, Stock & Barrel Auctions, used with permission.

Figure 5: Colt Model 1877 Lightning with nickel-plated finish and pearl grips.
Photo courtesy of Merz Antique Firearms, used with permission.

Figure 6: Colt Model 1878 Double Action Frontier with nickel-plated finish and ivory
grips. Photo courtesy of James Kattner collection, used with permission.

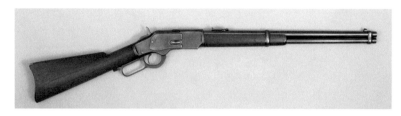

Figure 7: Winchester Model 1873 carbine, caliber .44 WCF. Author's collection.

Figure 8: Winchester Model 1873 rifle on top, caliber .44 WCF. Winchester Model 1876 rifle on bottom. Author's collection.

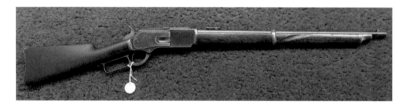

Figure 9: Winchester Model 1876 carbine. Photo courtesy of Merz Antique Firearms, used with permission.

Figure 10: Winchester Model 1886 carbine. Photo courtesy of Merz Antique Firearms, used with permission.

Figure 11: Winchester Model 1886 rifle. Photo courtesy of Merz Antique Firearms, used with permission.

Figure 12: Peabody-Martini sporting rifle. Photo courtesy of Merz Antique Firearms, used with permission.

Figure 13: Joe Elliot's custom Sharps Model 1874 sporting rifle. Photo courtesy of David Carter, used with permission. Photograph by Ron Paxton.

Figure 14: Sharps Model 1878 sporting rifle. Photo courtesy of Merz Antique Firearms, used with permission.

Figure 15: Cartridges from left: .40-60 WCF, .45-60 WCF, .45-70 Government, .45-90 WCF. Author's collection.

Figure 16: Cartridges from left: .38 Long Colt, .38 WCF, 44 WCF, .45 Colt.

Author's collection.

Figure 17: Top and side view of a box of Winchester-made .44 WCF cartridges.

Author's collection.

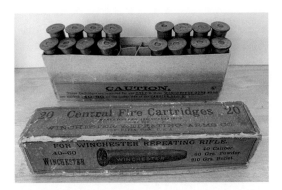

Figure 18: Top and side view of an open box of Winchester-made .40-60 WCF cartridges.

Author's collection.

Figure 19: Top view of a box of Winchester-made .45 Colt cartridges. Photo courtesy of Cam Gogsill collection, used with permission.

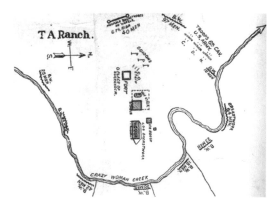

Figure 20: Map of the TA Ranch that shows the locations of the invaders and the posse surrounding them. *BW* stands for "breastwork" and shows the disposition of the posse members. Photo public domain.

# Index

Single Action Army revolver (SAA or Peacemaker) 2, 4, 15, 33, 34

## D

Davis, H. W. ("Hard Winter") 8

Davis, W. S. ("Quickshot") 22

De Billier, Frederic O. 19, 29, 32

double-action revolvers 3, 4, 12, 16, 18, 20, 26

Dudley, Jim 27

DuFran, Phil 22, 30, 31

Dunning, George 6, 24

## E

Elliot, Joe 4, 15, 16, 22, 30, 32, 38

## F

firearms

costs of 13

long arms/long guns 12, 15

by make, model, and serial number 29–32

surrender of 18–21

Foote, Robert 9, 11

Ford, Charles 19, 30, 31

Fort McKinney 1, 10, 27

Fraker, Harmon (AKA Old Dan Boone) 11

## G

Garrett, Buck 25, 30

Garrett, J. A. 16, 25, 30

gunmen, hired in Johnson County War 24–27

guns. *See* firearms; *specific models*

Guthrie, W. E. 19, 29, 31

## H

Hamilton, Alex 25, 29, 30

Harrison, Benjamin 10

Henry rifle 14

Hesse, Fred G. S. 8, 9, 14, 19, 29, 31

hired gunmen, in Johnson County War 24–27

Horner, Joe (AKA Frank M. Canton) 22

## I

Ijams, H. B. 6

Irvine, William C. ("Billy") 8, 10, 19

## J

Jim Gatchell Museum 11

Johnson, J. C. 25, 29, 32

Johnson County War

firearms used in 11–17

overview of 6–10

photo of invaders 33

## K

KC Ranch 8, 9, 11, 25

## L

Laberteaux, F. H. 19, 29, 31

Lightning. *See* Colt, Model 1877 Lightning

Little, William 25, 30

long arms/long guns 12, 15

Lowther, Alex 10, 27

## M

Martini. *See also* Peabody-Martini

McNally, M. A. 25, 30

Morrison, Ben 16, 22, 29, 31

Murray, Robert A. 1, 12, 28

Mynett, J. D. vii, 16, 26, 30, 31, 34

## O

octagon barrels 13, 15

Old Reliable Sharps single-shot rifle 15

Omnipotent 16

Printed in the United States
by Baker & Taylor Publisher Services